Grace

Thirty-Five Women Share Letters of Reflection to the Little Girl or Young Woman They Once Were

A compilation of letters presented by Tiffany M. Fincher, MSHS

Edited By

Aundrea L. Besst

Cover Illustrator

Justin Carey

Publisher

Inside Out Press

ISBN-13: 978-0-9992111-3-7

Back Cover Photo: Make-up

Rashia Williams

Back Cover Photography

Bill Montgomery

Table of Content

This book is dedicated to my grandmothers; Billy Hill and Julia Weathers.

Billy Hill   **Julia Weathers**

Acknowledgements

To my heavenly father, thank you for the vision you allowed me to see on that snowy January morning. My prayer is that this book honors you and makes you proud.

To each fearless woman who contributed to this body of work, with tremendous gratitude, I thank you for sharing your stories. Your letters are incredibly written, richly crafted, and beautifully moving. Women will be inspired by the insight revealed at the turn of each page. I pray that God opens special doors for each and every one of you.

To my husband, Shawn D. Fincher, my biggest supporter, encourager, and best friend. Thank you for allowing me the space to grow personally and professionally. Most of all, thank you for your unconditional love.

To my daughters, Kayla and Kamryn, my greatest inspiration. Early mornings, late nights, before and after work; I was committed to producing something that will be a gift to you one day. Thank you for being my personal cheerleaders throughout this journey.

To my father, Alvin Weathers Jr., you are the *BEST* father that I could ever ask for. Thank you for your wisdom, example of hard work, discipline, and the many sacrifices you've made over the years. Daddy, I love you.

To my mother, Marie A. Weathers, thank you for giving me life. Your love and encouragement mean the world to me. Thank you for supporting me in the endeavor of publishing this book. I've used every ounce of fire and determination inherited from you through each step of this process.

To my sister, Danielle M. Clark, a daring soul who challenged me to be BOLD in this one life we have to live. Thank you for being an extraordinary big sister. During your time here on this earth, you taught me many lessons. I know you are watching over me.

Introduction

BY TIFFANY M. FINCHER

"Your life is your story and the adventure ahead of you is the journey to fulfill your own purpose and potential."

-Kerry Washington

If you could send a letter to your younger self, what would it say? How many times have you said, "If I knew then what I know now"? If you are anything like me, you've probably said those words at least a million times.

One morning, I woke up early to pray and meditate before starting my day, as I do every morning. As I sat at the kitchen table, looking out of the window, my mind circled back to this familiar thought. As we mature, we experience several moments where we reflect on specific times in our lives. What if we could fast forward time and get advice from the women we have grown to be today?

Each contributor responded to the question: *If you could send a letter to your younger self, what would it say?* I pursued the answer to this question at a time in my life when I had a strong desire to glean from the wisdom of my grandmothers, whom I never had the chance to know. As strange as it might sound, I grieve their absence on this earth, mourn the fact that we've never met, and long for the chance to develop those critical relationships. I'm often told I carry the spirit of my grandmother, Julia Weathers, and the feistiness of my grandmother, Billy Hill. I wish I could visit them, pick up the phone to ask their advice, or inquire how they handled pivotal moments in their lives. After much thought, it really boiled down to wanting truth, transparency, and honesty about life. There will be times in life where we just want to be still, listen, and glean from the wisdom of our elders. From this space is where *Grace* was born.

God did something really special in connecting thirty- five divine women to share stories of strength, courage, and healing. One common thread among each co-author was the amount of healing that took place throughout the process. Not only did it birth individual healing; each personal story will be used as a catalyst for something much bigger than us.

Hold on to your seat. This is a "book of life", a collaboration written by thirty-five extraordinary women between the ages of 29-95 years old. They were brave enough to share letters of vulnerability and strength with the world. Each co-author is a woman who I highly respect and admire through relationships I have built personally and professionally. Fact! There is not a woman on this earth who does not have struggles, regrets, and QUESTIONS about life! If you are reading this book, at this very moment, many of the answers to some of your questions are being held in the palm of your hand. Each letter will show you that there will be times when life will blow the wind out of you! It's a part of the recipe that builds the women we are today. The best stories come from struggles. The seeds of your successes are in your trials, and praises will be birthed from your pain.

Live and Dance like Everyone is Watching

BY SANDY SAMPSON

"Your body is the temple of the Holy Spirit."

1COR 6:19

Beloved, I love you just the way you are. The Presence of God is looking at you and saying "You are my Beloved. You are my perfect idea. You are my Offspring of Infinite Potential. You are precious and divine. There is so much beauty in you, joy and love, harmony and power, peace, poise and confidence, prosperity, wealth, and abundance. All of these qualities are in you. Set them free, magnify them. You are the perfect one to live AND dance like everyone is watching."

You were conditioned to believe certain things early in life. You grew up with negative, mixed messages about your life and body. There were times you were called a "fast ass girl" by your parents because your body was shaped like a "brick house", as we call it. You were being judged for the way your body was designed. You didn't carry yourself in a negative way. You loved fashion, dancing, and being creative. You were taught that girl's bodies could lead the men in church into temptation, so cover up. That negatively affected you. You were afraid to wear certain clothing, thinking about what they would say about you. Your expression for creativity was deeply mistaken as rebellion and disobedience. Those around you can influence so many things like, how you view your body or your life. Every positive, negative, and in between comment can begin to change what that young, impressionable girl sees in the mirror. If this isn't understood, your self-esteem can and will be compromised for the worst. The spirit of comparison begins to creep in, and you feel shame, anxiety, and self-consciousness.

Some people may disapprove of your beautiful body, possibly due to concerns about culture and religious beliefs. Don't settle in that defeat. Your body is a God thing. Your body is the sacred temple of the Holy Spirit dripping in gold and honey. Embracing this is a choice you have to make each and every moment. This process has pushed you to fiercely remind yourself that you are valuable and worthy in your body. Remember your worth is not determined by your appearance. Your worth is not determined by your size. Your worth is not determined by your family's limiting beliefs. You are worthy simply because you exist. When they see you, they see The Omni Presence of

God in you. Know this! Be this! Be thankful and grateful for the miracle of your body. Stand in front of the mirror and bless your body – starting with your feet and legs, which allow you to keep standing and dancing, and ending with your head which gives you the brain power to execute the rhythm and beat of your life.

Sandy

Redline

BY CANDICE POPE

"Trust in the Lord with all my heart and in all my ways acknowledge Him, so he could direct my path."

Proverbs 3:5.

Hey girl,

Life is a journey, and more than anything, you have to remember to just TRUST THE PROCESS. Adapting to this mindset isn't going to be easy. It took you a while to get here, and you're still adjusting, but you're adjusting better than ever!

Between the ages of 28-29, you experienced and survived some tough terrain. Within the past ten years, you've experienced divorce, grief from divorce, grief from the death of a friend by suicide, men in and out of your life, promiscuity, home burglary and invasion, depression, anxiety, unstable living conditions, unemployment, insecurities, feelings of doubt and hopelessness, feelings of being unsure, anger, addiction, and more. You found yourself spiraling out of control, but while experiencing all of this, you never gave up on God.

You sank into a deep depression. You often found yourself crying and wanting to give up on life. You thought escaping from it all would make everything better. Once, you took a trip with your uncle to Atlanta, Georgia, and didn't want to return to Chicago. You had nothing to show for your life. You lived in a home that had just been robbed, and needed to be badly rehabbed. You lost your dog, had no job, and the only things you owned were clothes, cheap furniture, and a raggedy Chevy. You thought of just moving to Atlanta with your aunt and uncle and few friends. You wanted to stay, but when you prayed, God clearly said no. The depression took over when you returned home. You were sad and lonely. You drank a lot, almost every night. You partied a lot, and dated and slept with more than a few men. Through all of this, you continued to pray, read your word, and attend church. You listened to God and continued to pray for change. Although you weren't pleased with God's answer, you didn't give up. You began a daily workout routine and lost a ton of weight. You searched for jobs while on unemployment, and did hair, which was always a gift.

You began to practice evangelism, and started a Redline transportation ministry with a friend. You encouraged others who traveled via subway by singing Gospel songs and reading scripture. You spent many nights falling to your knees, eyes full of tears, and crying out to God to protect and guide you. You prayed for peace, a change for the better, and to experience love and joy. You were steadfast in your commitment to trusting God with your life.

He delivered you. God gave you joy, peace, a new vision, and provision. He gave you a new husband, who you met on Chicago's Redline transportation, two new jobs, a place of your own, and a new state of mind. You are seeing the things that you prayed for manifested right before your eyes, and there's plenty more to come! You got to move to Georgia after God answered your prayers. God said He had to mold and mature you. He wanted to equip you spiritually and emotionally before you relocated. He even blessed you with a husband who supported and shared your vision. All you had to do was believe and receive Proverbs 3:5. "TRUST IN THE LORD WITH ALL MY HEART AND IN ALL MY WAYS ACKNOWLEDGE HIM, SO HE COULD DIRECT MY PATH". You continue to do this every day and He continues to bless you. You are so grateful. Heed this advice and take it with you wherever you go. Always be encouraged.

Candice

Know Your Worth

BY NAKIA ROUNSAVILLE

"For I know the plans I have for you," declares the LORD, "plans to prosper you and not to harm you, plans to give you hope and a future."

Jeremiah 29:11 (NIV)

At the age of sixteen, you were smart, attractive, independent, and respectful to your elders. Although you had charisma, there was another side of you that loved the attention of men. Regardless if they were single or married, your goal was to obtain a relationship with someone older because you believed that was a sign of maturity and a well-established life.

Attending high school and working part-time at an insurance company, you started dating men and exploring things that were too advanced for someone your age; going to adult parties and lying to your parents about your whereabouts.

During this time, all you truly cared about was yourself. No feelings were involved in these relationships. There was no true connection with anyone you were dating. You almost considered it a game. Everyone was different. Some fell in love with you, and if they did you would begin to limit your time with them or completely cut off all communication. Others just enjoyed if you gave them time out of your day.

After graduation, you decided to work full time. You began to date someone that you met at a bar who you were attracted to physically and mentally. Of course, he was older, but you felt confident that this would be a relationship you never experienced and you both could grow together.

Five years later, you were pregnant with his child. You were in love, until you gave him the news about your unexpected new bundle of joy. He denied being the father, and accused you of cheating to avoid the responsibility of being a parent. It was devastating. After all, this was the first guy you thought you fell in love with. You allowed yourself to become vulnerable with this man. You couldn't consider terminating the pregnancy because when you finally received the pregnancy results, it was too late.

You weren't quite prepared to be a mother. After the delivery of your beautiful daughter, it was time to speak with your former boyfriend about co-parenting and assisting with support. The conversation was short and direct – he wanted very minimal interaction with her.

Now a single mother, you had to do what was best for your child. After receiving a letter from the court requiring DNA testing, you totally removed yourself from that relationship, and did not settle until she received financial support. You had to push past the hurt. It wasn't an easy process, but necessary.

At times, you felt lonely and foolish because the person that you thought loved you appeared to be a stranger. You cried yourself to sleep, releasing some of the pain that you felt because you still had feelings for this man. I knew that I couldn't return to a person that denied your child. She was too young and precious to understand the situation. You had to set an example for your daughter.

Years passed, and her father suggested getting back together- but you declined. By that time, you realized neither you, nor your daughter deserved the hurt and pain he caused. You refused to put her at risk of disappointment.

Love has so many dynamics. It's been said that "love is the most powerful force in the universe". As I reflect on the past, I would say I didn't know my true worth. I deserved much more than I settled for. Self-gratification was more important to me.

Knowing your worth doesn't happen overnight. Sometimes it takes years of experiences, lessons, heartaches, and prayer until you understand who you are and what you're worth. We are called to be virtuous women.

Proverbs 31: 10-12 (NLT version) states: Who can find a virtuous and capable wife? She is more precious than rubies. Her husband can trust her, and she will greatly enrich his life. She brings him good, not harm, all the days of her life.

We as women are powerful, don't allow anyone to speak negatively of your purpose because of your past mistakes.

Nakia

The Dream: Above and Abroad

BY DR JANELLE HADLEY

"God is within her, she will not fall."

Psalm 46.5

Dearest Janelle,

Medicine has played a huge role in your life from your mother getting a kidney transplant while you were in the 7th grade, to your niece being born prematurely and you visiting her in the hospital daily for 3 months while in high school. Both times, you were unsure of what was going on, but you always asked the transplant team and NICU staff questions respectively. Sometimes there was fear, but most times there was intrigue. In the latter moments, filled with hospital sounds and monitor notifications, you found an unknown comfort.

Fast forward to the age of 26. You are gainfully employed at a reputable university with a predictable and steady career. However, you have elected to forfeit everything and exchange it for a life filled with uncertainty. This journey will be coupled with multiple unforeseen hardships, as chasing this dream requires you to venture off to a foreign land to study medicine. Before you go, there are three things I so desperately want to share with you. I hope you can hear me.

1. Seek mentorship and guidance.

   You have convinced yourself that networking is something you are not good at. You are used to doing things alone without consult. But this??!!! You absolutely CANNOT do on your own. It is crucial to have individuals in your life who are exactly where you wish to be especially considering no one in your family has done this before. Making these connections will be integral to your success. These individuals will not only help guide you, but also provide encouragement when you need it most. Start as early as POSSIBLE!

2. You are stronger than you know!

   You have questioned whether or not you are smart enough for this. And truth be told, studying medicine has absolutely NOTHING to do with how smart you are. Your journey relies heavily on your tenacity, discipline, and resilience. You will fail so many quizzes and tests that you lose count. Your mother will need to have another major surgery, but you will not be there. You will postpone having a mate, family, and home of your own while your counterparts post about these things daily. But one thing is for sure! Your ability to continue despite it being easier to quit is undoubtedly amazing. Nothing will stop you, and will rise up to be stronger than you ever could imagine.

3. Your courage has inspired me!

    Sometimes us younger folk don't get much credit. We get labeled as rebellious and fastidious millennials, but you? You have inspired me! I mean, at this current age of 32, I don't think I would have what it takes to do what you did. You left all that you ever knew for a dream that wasn't guaranteed. You emptied your savings to invest in yourself. You did what was unexpected. And for that, you are a trailblazer and merely at the age of 26! It is refreshing. You have certainly helped me remember what courage looks like in human form.

    In closing, my prayer is that you found these lessons to be useful. And once you use them, share them with others so they can not only avoid some pitfalls, but also recognize their power. I love you, and I can't wait to see you GLOW!

    P.S. You will Match and become a resident at the same hospital you spent months at visiting your premature niece. The ultimate fullest circle moment!

    Love always,

    Janelle

Mr. Wonderful

BY DEBORAH GARY

"What no eye has seen, nor ear heard, nor the heart of man imagined, what God has prepared for those who love him"

1 Corinthians 2:9

Dear Debbie,

This marriage IS different. You say you married him because he loves you just the way you are, but he doesn't know you very well, does he? And even if he did, we all should make an effort to continuously grow until we die.

Right now, you are ready to give up. You are emotionally exhausted and depressed. You are asking people for a good counselor but saying, "It's for a friend." You don't understand why your three worded prayers to God, "Please change him!" should really be, "Please change ME!"

This husband does not want to control you like you think the first one did. While being a single mom, you vowed never to be controlled again. You never wanted to be dependent on another man, or anyone else for that matter. You aren't even fighting hard for child support because you're thinking, "I got this." But God helped you anyway. He sent you a King. A King that will only be revealed when you act like a Queen. You will feel richer, supported, protected, and more secure *after* you assume your role as a Queen because being controlled and being taken care of are two different things. Right now, it's like you've entered into a new season of summer warmth, but you are still clinging to your fur coat and thick leggings. Still sipping on warm drinks, and sweating profusely while bitching about how hot you are. You must shed the old you. It's not just you and your two boys anymore. You don't have to be the head anymore. Yes, you are strong, but you were built to be the helpmate.

You must stop bad mouthing your husband. Sitting in the car to have a private venting session with your girlfriend to call your husband an idiot, only makes you Mrs. Idiot. You know life and death are in the power of the tongue. So, speak life into your marriage. Move forward. Trust that your husband is God's gift to you. Begin to shed the layers of cold winter, and feel the warmth of the sun of righteousness rise with healing in its rays. Refer to your loving husband as Mr.

Wonderful and mean it. Then, experience the positive energy that will make you Mrs. Wonderful. Be prepared to receive what your eyes have not seen, what your ears have not heard, and what you heart will feel...LOVE.

Sincerely,

Mrs. Wonderful

A Love Letter to "Little Kim"

BY KIMBERLY COSEY

"Are not five sparrows sold for two pennies? And not one of them is forgotten before God. Why, even the hairs of your head are all numbered. Fear not; you are of more value than many sparrows."

Luke 12:6-7

You've questioned GOD on several occasions regarding His perception on the amount of strength that He gave you. You have often felt weak throughout your life, pretending to be this strong Black woman. You can accept this now, but your biggest weakness was men. Unfortunately, your issues with men began with your biological father pulling a disappearing act at the age of two, and you wanting to know why. You had questions that needed answers. Answers that were as distant as your biological father. You were in a long-term relationship with your now ex-husband, and you felt taken for granted and strung along. As your thirtieth birthday approached, the same questions ran through your mind. "How can a man have a child and live on this earth without knowing them?" "Kimberly, why are you sitting around waiting for this man to marry you?" You decided that thirty needed to be the year you answered at least one of those questions. So, you began to search for your biological father. You'd finally found a working number that was attached to him, and you spoke to a nice lady that said she knew him, but he no longer lived in Illinois. So, you did what you do best. You wrote him a very long letter, hoping he'd receive it, and answer your questions. Questions that needed answers, and answers that felt a little bit closer to your ears and heart. Your mother wasn't happy that you were digging up old bones, but only a person in your position could understand that you were taking steps to your own healing. Who knew you would need healing from something you never had, from someone you never knew. You anxiously awaited a reply, only to receive your letter, returned to sender, a few weeks later. You were crushed and felt abandoned all over again. You hated yourself for allowing him to hurt you. Again, you had so many questions. Questions that needed answers, and answers that remained unclear, unreal, and unfulfilled.

The things that I would tell "Little Kim" at the age of twenty-nine are many, but I'll share a few that could have been life altering.

Don't have expectations of others; expecting things from others is a set up for disappointment. So, expect nothing, but do appreciate things that are done out of love.

Love yourself the way that GOD loves you. Love your skinny legs and arms. Appreciate your slim frame, your complexion, the confusing curls adorned upon your head, the large teeth in your mouth. For one day, that slim frame will bring life into this world. Your skin will glow with GOD's purpose, those curls will no longer be confusing, but a crown of glory, and those teeth will accompany a smile that people remember most about you. Loving yourself as royalty will allow you to receive the pure and genuine love from your future King.

Follow your dreams. You don't have to live up to others' expectations of you. Don't feel guilty if you choose to follow your own path, and not the path everyone wants you to follow. This is your life to live. You see "Little Kim", you're smart, and GOD blessed you with visions and talents that only you can develop. The spectators of your life won't know what to do with the gifts that GOD made special for you. You're the only one with the passion and knowledge to birth these gifts. These gifts will one day help people develop businesses. Your perseverance and sometimes doubted strength will fight for your child's education.

Finally, have patience with yourself. Embrace your short comings, and work to improve yourself. You are a garden that needs maintenance to experience growth and to emit beauty into this world. Kimberly, try not to be too hard on yourself...give yourself grace.

Love,

Grace

Kim

Full of Life

BY CHEREESE KING

"Deal with yourself as an individual worthy of respect, and make everyone else deal with you the same way."

Nikki Giovanni

Hello Suzy Q,

You've done so well dealing with the challenges you've already overcome at your age. You are smart, with a great sense of humor, and a smile that shines brightly for everyone to see. Those qualities will serve you well in your life.

There are several attributes that I now know as a wiser woman, which can help you tremendously moving forward in life. Those attributes are self-discipline, self-respect, intelligence, courteousness, and love .

Life has been challenging, and I know this could've been prevented early. Prevention is key. You've been diagnosed with a disease called Lupus. Lupus is an autoimmune disorder where your body's immune system attacks your organs. It's been very hard living with it. Severe joint pain, rashes, bleeding and kidney issues. All of our youth was consumed with battling this disease. Now, we can prevent this from ever happening with self-discipline and removing those negative influences. Your diet and mental health are very important, and have a large impact on your health in the future. So does the drama, it's negative. So, microwaving that bacon all the time. Stop doing it! The bacon and egg sandwiches and other unhealthy foods every day, must stop! It affects your health negatively. Replace it with fruits and vegetables. Stay active. Jog. It's good exercise you can do anywhere. Start running again, you like it, and you're good at it.

Use self-control, and don't say everything that comes to mind. Verbal abuse is just as bad as physical abuse. Stop being argumentative. Say please and thank you like you were taught at home. It doesn't make you a nerd. Be polite and courteous. It goes a long way. Smoking will be introduced to you soon. Don't do it! You don't need to appear to be cool.

You're smart, focus on your school work. Use your brain, and go to college. No one told you before, but you can have the time of your life and meet amazing people, all while learning. It will make your life richer, culturally and literally. Take business, get interested in school, and leave those bad boys alone. You are smart and beautiful, they just want to take your honey! You seek the attention of your father. Call him, and stop seeking attention from men. When parents separate, it's hard on a father to call or visit the house of the woman that despises

27

him. Reach out to your father more because you need him. Stop blaming him, he really does love you.

Elevate your mind. Show love, and love who you are because you are a very strong, smart and clever. Use it to your advantage, and think of your future. Have fun and stop trying to be grown, enjoy being a kid. You'll be glad you did. Trust me.

Lots of love,

Chereese

Life after Death

BY STEPHANIE DUKES

"Blessed are they that mourn: for they shall be comforted."

Matthew 5:4

On June 16, 2004, in Fort Worth, TX, at the age of 39, the day started as any other day for you. There was no indication that it would be the day that would forever change your life. You prepared for the day by spending some quality time with your husband of 12 years and your two beautiful children Lauren (8) and Christopher (13). Your children, along with other children from your church were preparing to participate in the National Missionary Baptist Convention of American Drill Team competition. Following a long day of meetings, you all wanted a few minutes to relax before the competition. So, you proceeded to your hotel room and the children went swimming in the hotel pool, which you found out later was closed.

So, you advised your husband to take the children across the street to what you believed was a park, but it was the Fort Worth Water Garden. The water garden had a cascading waterfall that would attract any child on a hot summer day and it did. Here lies where your life changed forever.

Your husband, son, daughter, along with another child, all drowned. We don't know the time or hour the Lord will call us home, but you weren't prepared to lose your entire family. You had no idea what to do, who to talk to, where to go, or how you would continue your life without them. You were lost. They were a part of your heart and soul. Living without them wasn't an option, but GOD, who knows all and sees all, is a rewarder of those who seek Him.

He gave you a chance to start over. A chance to regain some normalcy in your life with the adoption of three children Tyra, Dillaun and Emerald. So, my words of encouragement are "Blessed are they that mourn: for they shall be comforted" Matthew 5:4.

Stephanie

KIND - SMART – IMPORTANT

BY LAUREN JACKSON

"God is within her she will not fail."

Psalms 46:5

You were 25 years old when you had "the talk" with your father. No, it wasn't the talk about the birds and the bees. It was the talk about acknowledging the fact that you were indeed his daughter. You had been trying to have this talk with him for quite some time. However, due to his own fear, he came up with countless excuses about why he was unable to meet with you. But finally, the day arrived.

You were so nervous, yet somewhat excited. Deep down, you were hoping this would be the day you would finally get to be Daddy's little girl. You thought it would be a beautiful start to a brand new relationship between the two of you. Truth be told, you already knew he was your father from a very young age. Chop it up to amazing intuition, but you knew he was way more than just your "Mom's Friend". That didn't matter to you. You were willing to forgive and forget if that meant having the opportunity to actually have your own dad in your life and not constantly relying on the support of your many father figures.

This isn't to downplay the crucial impact they had on your life. There aren't enough "thank yous" in the world to show your admiration and appreciation for the way they stepped up, attempting to fill voids you felt being a Daddyless Daughter. You yearned to have those father daughter talks and extra emotional support. You ultimately craved the attention from the man who was supposed to be your first love instead of your first example of heartbreak.

On the meeting day, you found yourself looking at your father realizing that the relationship you always prayed and hoped for would never come to pass. Throughout your meeting, you were able to gain insight on why he chose not to be fully in your life. Most were mere excuses. Others were clear indications that he just wasn't ready to take full ownership or even come to terms with how much he hurt you over the years. It was then that you came to the conclusion that your father was incapable of giving you the love you needed in order to make it in this world.

Was it heartbreaking? Absolutely. But was it necessary? Yes.

I know how much it hurts you when the ones you love most aren't always willing to serve you the way you need them to. You figured, if you could always support them, be their go to person, prove yourself, and ultimately suspend your own happiness for theirs, at some point they would reciprocate that same grace to you. Unfortunately, you had to learn the hard way, not everyone is capable or willing to show you love like you show them. And that's okay.

When I look at you now, I see how you used your special calling of helping others to deflect from the unhappiness you felt on a daily basis. You wore a mask of perfection. You always had to make the right decision, or the consequences of failure and rejection would become your true identity. Warm and friendly on the outside, hallow and empty on the inside. Those feelings of unworthiness, not good enough, not pretty enough, and definitely not smart enough followed you everywhere you went.

You tried not to blame your parents for these feelings, but this only led to an internal battle of hurt, confusion, and anger. They played a major role in your low self-esteem and poor self-image, but not intentionally. You see, you may have been a surprise to your parents, but God knew what He was doing when He created you. Bright eyed, bushy tailed, ambitious, and ready to set this world on fire!
As you continue to grow and become wiser, you begin to realize both of your parents are simply human. They've made plenty of mistakes, and you were just an innocent bystander at their attempt to getting life

"right". I know it crushes your spirit when they don't take ownership of their flaws and how it impacts you. Please understand, they could only love you with the knowledge and capacity they had. Whether they want to admit it, you actually taught them how to love themselves better!

I know you wish your relationship with them was more meaningful, but God has always kept a hedge of protection around you. The people in your village stepped up in areas that your parents could not. Remember, you are not your parents' mistakes. Nor will you repeat the cycle of unhealthy relationships. You don't have to settle for love or tolerate abuse for the sake of gaining validation.

Realize there's a difference between being alone and being lonely. You've experienced massive amounts of loneliness. Just know, with a lot of love, support, prayers, therapy, and most importantly having God's hand upon you, a shift takes place! You will finally realize, you were always enough!

Your compassion, grace, personality, and even your gorgeous body have always been your special spark. Your smile alone can turn a gloomy day, bright. Not to mention, when you speak, your presence commands the room. Everyone takes note!

Before I let you go, I want you to remember 3 things you learned from a movie called The Help. These simple, yet powerful statements will carry you far in life, and will help you serve the world in incredible ways.

1.) You is KIND! - Your kindness sets you apart. It is the very thing that draws others to you. While extending kindness to them, always remember to show that same kindness to yourself. Never let other people or your circumstances make you think that being kind is a form weakness. In fact, it takes great strength! By extending kindness to yourself, it allows others to do the same.

2.) You is SMART! - You literally have nothing to prove to ANYONE! Some things can't be learned from a book. You, my dear, are a voracious learner. You have brains for days. Your book smarts, street smarts, and the ability to intuitively connect with God and those around you is truly unfathomable. No need to compare your journey with anyone else's. Your wisdom speaks to all generations.

3.) You is IMPORTANT! - Never dim your light to accommodate others. Your greatness shines so brightly. You naturally glow with God's radiance. Own that part of you. Be proud of your many accomplishments. Be present for every high, low, and in-between moment of God's plan for you.

There is so much more I want to pour into you little lady. If I could leave you with one last pearl of wisdom, it would be to embrace your shortcomings and know that you are the apple of God's eye. You are the Princess growing into the Queen He always created you to be!

Love You Always,
Lauren

I Wish I Could Have Told You

BY LISA REDD- WAITS

"For you created my inmost being; you knit me together in my mother's womb I praise you because I am fearfully and wonderfully made; I know that full well."

Psalms 139:13-14(NIV)

Dear Sweet 11-year-old Lisa:

All of your life you have yearned for a sister, a friend, a confidant. Someone to share your hopes, dreams, aspirations, and fears with. I wish I could have told you that one day you would have people in your life to fill the void of the loneliness you've always felt. You will one day be comfortable in the skin you are in, and love yourself unconditionally, flaws and all.

Growing up with six brothers, no sisters or friends, you craved for the bond that you felt only a sister could provide. Although you and your

37

Mom loved each other, you weren't very close. However, that would change as you get older. I wish I could have told you that.

One Saturday morning, you felt the loneliness was unbearable, you decided to take as many Tylenol you could find, trying to numb the unhappiness. Suicide, nor death, ever crossed your mind, you simply wanted to sleep the sadness away. I'm beyond thankful that God had a plan for your life, and your loving parents rescued you. They provided the assistance you needed through therapy, family discussions, prayer, and lots of love. That one Saturday morning changed your life.

I wish I could have told you that you are beautiful, and the loneliness and sadness would soon fade away. I want you to know that you are perfect just the way you are; quiet, shy and soft spoken. It's okay to be yourself! The Sister/Friends that belong in your life would come and value your friendship. You will not be a "Sister-less Sister". You will have a tribe of powerful women in your life that will support, encourage, uplift, and pray for you. You will be a sister to many sisters, and the bond that you are so desperately seeking will one day be manifested in your life.

My dear sweet Lisa, the emptiness you felt as a child will make you appreciate and value your friendships, have compassion for people, and constantly want to serve those in need. You will grow and mature into a wonderful woman, wife, mother, grandmother, daughter, sister and friend. God's purpose for your life is greater than you could have ever imagined. Enjoy your journey! I wish I could have told you that you are loved, always and forever....

Lisa

Embrace Your Journey

BY KIMBERLY PACE

"I know the plans I have for you, declares the Lord, plans to prosper you and not harm you, plans to give you hope and a future."

Jeremiah 29:16

My Dearest Kimberly,

Embrace who you are. Kimberly, you are a young beautiful girl in the seventh grade. You've hit a growth spurt, and now you are taller than your friends and classmates. You feel awkward. The sleeves on your shirts are always too short. You frequently bump your knees on the desk...ouch! You outgrew your bike. Nobody makes tall pants! You are thinking, why me? You hate being awkward and tall.

Kimberly, stand up straight. You were meant to be tall in stature. EMBRACE your height, it is one of the attributes that adds to your beauty. Use those legs to walk a walk of confidence! Walk tall in the lane that was created just for you. Love your 5'9 frame. In your twenties, you started to appreciate your shape and long legs, but you also started to compare yourself to your peers in other ways. You began to ask yourself questions like;"Why don't I have what my peers have? Why am I the last to have my own place? Why am I the last single friend? Why is my career moving slowly?" You felt as if you were being left behind in every important aspect of your life?

When you were 29, you worked a second job that allowed you to work evenings on the weekends. You lived at home until you were 32 years old, and hated it! You felt like you were failing, but decided you needed to make more money in order to save more. It helped you pay off debit and save money to purchase your first home. At 32 years old, you moved away from home, and became a homeowner. You were so proud of yourself! Time helps us to see things differently. Time also helps us to see things through more mature eyes. If I could have stepped into the future and saw where you would be, I would have encouraged you to understand this is YOUR process. You are going to have everything your heart desires. Embrace your journey.

You have so many more years to live, and so many experiences to add to your journey. When you find yourself on the road to comparison, STOP and change directions. The words you speak to yourself will be some of the most important words you will ever hear. Pay attention and discipline your thoughts and your mouth to only speak positivity.

Embrace who you are, and appreciate where you are and where you are going. Remember your journey is about you. The creator gave it to you. Life is about finding YOUR own way. Shine in it, and Embrace the Journey!

Love Always,
Kim

Purpose and Strength

BY CHERYL L. BAKER

"I was and still am called according to his purpose."

Romans 8:28

My dear Cheryl,

I see you...

You, are a very special young lady. You may not think so at this very moment, but you are.

The difficult times that you, your brother, and your mom have gone through and will go through, have and will serve a purpose. Hard times such as having to move from your childhood home because the rent becomes too much for your mom to afford, will have a purpose. Hard times such as having to move again because the one-bedroom rental unit your mom could afford for you, your brother, herself, and your sister (when she moves back in), becomes uninhabitable due to the owners moving out in the middle of the night, in the dead of winter without paying the utilities (even though your mom paid the rent) leaving your family with nowhere to go, will have a purpose. Difficult times such a having your family split up (you to one friend's home, and your brother and mother to another), just to have a place to live, will have a purpose. These experiences, others from your past, and even more from your future will create life-sustaining nuggets of hope as well as mental-fortitudes of peace that you will digest over and over again, providing sustenance for you and those who hear your story. So, don't be afraid, my dear. You are not alone and there is a purpose.

You are not alone.

When you sit at the kitchen table doing your homework and cannot understand why your dad doesn't live with you or help take care of you or protect you, it is okay, you are not alone. When you wonder why your dad doesn't love you like the other kids' dads love them, it is okay, there is a purpose – you are not alone.

I want you to know that you, young lady, have another Father. You haven't met Him yet, but He knows all about you. This Father will live with you. He will protect you and take care of you. He will love you like no one else can or will. He has already demonstrated His love for you even though you don't know Him yet.

Cheryl, as you get older, never try to fill the void in your heart with the temporary "love" of a boy or man. The love you've been missing and are longing for can only come from your other Father, your Heavenly Father. He is watching over you all the time. He is with you all the time. He loves you all the time. Him… you can trust.

An Adult's Reflection:

I became engaged to be married in January 1990, I was 21 years old. Seven months later, in August 1990 at the age of 22, I was married.

I loved my husband, and had always dreamt of being married, having a family and doing it "right". I was a younger Christian at the time, and I wanted to be the best biblical wife and eventually, the best biblical mother, I could possibly be. I really wanted God to be happy with me – to be pleased with me. So, I dedicated myself to my husband and my church, and later my husband, my children, and my church. You see, I loved reading God's word, and wanted to do what He said for me to do. However, somewhere along the way, and it is not God's fault, but I lost me. Did I ever really know "me"? After all, did I ever really take the time to get to know me? When did it happen? Why did it happen? I'd married my high school sweetheart just 4 years after graduation. So, it must have happened rather early in my new-found married and ministry life.

In my short time of being a Christian, I'd been taught that the church came before anything and anyone else. Yet, I was conflicted. I thought that family came first, which included loving God himself. Later, I was told that I, as a person, only mattered because of, whom I married; that people only tolerated me because of who my husband was; and that people only liked me because of him. I was often sad and depressed, and wondered what the purpose of these additional difficult times could possibly be.

However, later, through faith and reading God's word, I came to understand, believe, receive and know, that I too am fearfully and wonderfully made (Psalm 139:4). I came to realize that I too, was created for and with a purpose. Everything I had been allowed to experience, came as no surprise to God, my Heavenly Father, but that the opposite was true. God had given me the strength to go through all of those things because HE was causing them all to work together for my good because I love him. I was and still am called according to his purpose (Romans 8:28).

The way may be tough, but you are strong and there is a purpose.

Love,

Cheryl

It Gets Better

BY DR. KISHA ROBERTS- TABB

"She is clothed with strength and dignity, and she laughs without fear of the future."

Proverbs 31:25

Dear Kisha,

The first thing I would like to tell you is that things will get better. You're only fifteen, you have a lifetime to go. I know that for most of your childhood you felt like a foreign object trying to fit into a normal space. Unbeknownst to you, so was everyone else. What is normal? Everyone's normal is different. Your normal includes an addicted mother, and very strict father. I'm sure you thought your situation was different, but most of your friends' parents suffer from addiction as well. Your mom's addiction has nothing to do with you. There's nothing more you could do. You can't be a better daughter. You cannot love her more than you do right now. In fact, she knows how much you love her, despite your anger. It wasn't your fault she left. Addiction is an illness. Over the years, you all will create memories that you will never forget. I know you don't think so now, but her life's experiences will impact and guide all of your life's decisions. The very thing you lacked from her, you will pour into your own daughter. The older you get, you will learn to carry your mother's confidence. Believe it or not, you really did learn a lot from her. Tell her you love her as much as you can because sooner than later you will only be able to do so in your dreams. Be more understanding. There are so many things about your mom's life that you are unaware of. In her death, you will remember the things that everyone loved about her but you were too angry to see then. Your dad is pretty cool as well. The lessons and all of the punishments actually paid off. I know he always seemed to be doing too much, but it's actually just what you needed. Between me and you, he thought you were doing too much as well. As you get older, you will realize that disappointing him kept you out of a lot of trouble. Your annoying little sister will one day become your best friend. I know you think she prefers her friends over you, but I bet if you ask her, she thinks the same about you.

I know you hear the whispers, and the things that are being said about you. Guess what? The girls with so much to say about you, deep down really want to be just like you. Your Afrocentric style seems so different than everyone else. You like your braids and wooden earrings, and so do they. Unfortunately, no one ever told them that you don't have to bring others down to make yourself feel better. The

African Medallion that your Dad gave you is actually dope, and before you know it everyone will be wearing them. In fact, they will come back in style every few years. Even though you think your breasts are way too big, they will catch up with the rest of your body before you know it. You may not see your beauty, but they do. Therefore, the chatter is just a reflection of our inability to compliment each other as females. There's no need to try to fit in, you're pretty cool just the way you are. Remember where you are now, one day your daughter will be in the same space. Recognize what you need right now and offer it to her when she needs it.

This break up you are experiencing is one of many; you get better at it each time. You don't even know yourself, therefore you don't know if you even like him. When you look back, you will ask yourself "what was I thinking?" Remember, these relationships are only practice runs. Take what you need to learn from each of them and get rid of what you don't need. There is a man that will love you, marry you, and treat you like a queen. So, make sure you know how to wear a crown.

Be fearless, love yourself first, and smile more. There is so much more to your life than your right now.

Love,

Kisha

Rejection is a Building Block for Trail Blazers

BY GLORI BOND

"For I know the plans I have for you, declares the Lord, plans to prosper you and not to harm you, plans to give you hope and a future."

Jeremiah 29:11

Little Glori, I wish I could tell you how dangerous it is when the enemy has more intel about what lies in you than you. Do you remember that time when you were eight, and your aunt told you that you were not as pretty as your cousins, and that you didn't have the same grade of hair as them? This was the seed of rejection and self-consciousness being planted. Do you remember when your grandfather called you up to sing a solo, and one of the women in the church raised all kinds of hell, asking "why does she always have to sing?", saying "no one wants to hear her", and speculating that you were only getting chosen because you were the pastor's granddaughter. There was nothing special about you. These were the seeds of fear, unworthiness,

50

and self-doubt being planted. You learned to perform after that to ensure that they liked you, instead of ministering from the heart. Finally, I'm sure you remember that time when you finally got the courage to tell your mother you were molested at eight, and she begin to laugh uncontrollably. In that moment, you felt violated all over again. The seed of isolation and abandonment was rooted even deeper in your soul. What if I told you that the attacks, the betrayals, the pains, the violation you experienced would be a launching pad and place of healing and restoration for women that you would come in contact with. You see, the rejection that was sent to break you is really what built you. It trained you to walk alone, to trust in God alone, and not the opinion of man. You were affirmed in the heavens, and there was nothing anyone else could do about it. You had to rely on your faith when God gave you an assignment that others would not understand. The rejection you experienced caused you to have thick skin. It allowed you to plow through adversity, disappointment, obstacles, and trials. God's grace would not allow you to have a callous heart. It is very easy to go on paths that have already been blazed, but there are those like you who have to go ahead to clear the path. You may experience wounds, set-backs and discouragement along the way, but you were built for this. Everything about your life was intentional and purposeful. It was carefully interwoven into the fabric of the women who were to come after you. Do not waste time trying to prove your worth to people who have no concept of value. Know that what you carry is so precious and invaluable that you have to be cautious about who receives access to you. Go forth, be great, be whole, be healed, and blaze trails.

Sincerely,

Glori

Accept You ... Others Have!

BY CYNTHIA KEEL

"Keep me safe, O God, I've run for dear life to you. I say to GOD, "Be my Lord!" Without you, nothing makes sense."

Psalm 16:1-2 MSG

Hey Cynthia,

So, you're enjoying high school at Chicago Vocational, eh? I see that you're a passionate, diehard Christian. How awesome! I want you to have fun without judgement. Enjoy your love for Jesus, and enjoy being a teenager! You like boys, they're cute (well some of them are). You doubt your own beauty, comparing yourself to the cheerleaders and Pom-Pom girls. You feel like you don't measure up because your smarts didn't get you on the Senior Girls Council. That fall the other day, off the balance beam during gym, in front of the entire class didn't help your feelings of being awkward and clumsy... just not good enough. Don't you find it ironic though that the sports jocks invite you to sit with them at lunch, and they know you carry your Bible on top of your books? They ask you about your faith because they don't understand. You enjoy their inquiries about what interests you, but just can't embrace that they accept you for who you are and what you stand for. So, when you attend class reunions years later and are complimented for looking great because, in your classmates' words, "you didn't get caught up in all of the things we were doing," you will realize there was an unspoken respect for your stance. Be true to you! God is preserving you for the journey ahead to bring others into the awareness of who He really is. Relax, and enjoy the journey. Don't take yourself too seriously, and don't take everything so personally. You're going somewhere, and you're going to be just fine. You'll grow into the uniqueness of you — the fearfully and wonderfully made creation of Almighty God. You'll realize that you don't have to hide, dumb yourself down, or shy away from those who are different. Stop comparing yourself to others, and enjoy who you are! Get excited about who you'll become! Your future is bright. God is preserving you for His glory!

With buckets of love and hugs,
The You You're Becoming

Rewards and Consequences

BY SERITA LOVE

"If you fail to plan, you plan to fail."

Abraham Lincoln

Serita,

Life is no joke, but you are going to soar! People are going to love you because of your personality, and willingness to support others on their journey towards success. People aren't going to love you for the same reason, and that's okay! Allow me to provide you with a cheat sheet for your growth and development to avoid a few pitfalls in life.

You are going to attract so many amazing things in life, but be very careful. Before you commit to ANYTHING, do your research. There will always be rewards and/or consequences to everything you dedicate your time and energy to. I advise you to go after things that are beneficial. If there is no benefit to how you feel or how you prosper, then it may not be a good idea to get involved. What you commit yourself to should assist you in becoming a better person.

Many times in life, you will want to vent to people. Here is a word of advice, keep certain things to yourself. Before you reveal who you are to people remember there are always rewards or consequences. Everyone does not deserve to know everything about you. Keep this rule close especially until you get to know a person well enough to share your vulnerability. Trust me, I know this from experience. I've considered someone a good friend. I really thought I could tell them everything about me. I was wrong. I thought the feeling was mutual. Once again, I was wrong. We had never had an argument. To my knowledge, we never even had a disagreement. However, I learned how that person truly felt about me from someone else. I was hurt. I was disappointed. I felt betrayed. But, I later realized that I had to take some of the responsibility for exposing myself. This was merely one of those life lessons that changed the way I viewed things.

Your words have power! Be positive, and speak positivity into your life and the lives of those around you. If you wake up with a bad attitude, you will have a bad day. If you wake up with a great attitude, make it a great day. Sometimes you will have bad thoughts. As long as you don't say those words out loud, you have the power to adjust or erase those beliefs. If you pride yourself on progress, then having a positive mindset will be the key to your success. Encourage people to be their best. Build them up. Support them. Everything you put out into this world will come back to you as you give it. You are in control in more ways than you can ever imagine! You are smart. You are confident. If you take heed to these words, you will see everything and everyone in front of you a little differently. To proceed with caution doesn't require you to be afraid, it simply requires you to be alert. Keep those antennas up, baby girl.

I encourage you to plan out your future success. Tomorrow isn't promised, but if it does come, you want to be prepared. Get organized and map out your goals. What type of future do you see yourself having? Break down those goals. Understand that you will get frustrated sometimes, and things will not always go as planned. I firmly believe that if you can think it, then it is your responsibility to make it happen. Most people take their talents to the grave. You are not most people.

I want to tell you so much, but the best thing I can leave you with is, trust yourself. You will be challenged differently, and it will hurt. You will experience some things that you won't believe you deserve to experience. Oddly enough, these challenges will show you that you can overcome anything. Adversity is your super power. No one can take your strength away from you. With your unyielding faith, grit, and tenacity, you will always figure things out.

There is NOTHING you cannot do.

Girl, you've got this!

Serita

Don't Worry…Be Happy

BY JACQUELINE HORBROOK

"Every day I get to do something I love and make an impact on people's lives."

Amber Pence

Jackie,

Imagine flying at an altitude of 12,000 feet, seeing friends make the deliberate, intentional decision to jump with their parachutes neatly and functionally assembled. While yours is scattered on the floor with the "How To" instructions missing. As you get older, you will hear a lot of people ask you one important question, "What do you want to be when you grow up?" This question haunted you for a very long time. Most of your friends had their whole lives planned out before the 2nd grade. You, on the other hand, could not pick one. So instead, you chose to change your answer each time someone asked. This went on all the way through high school and into college.

Looking back on those times, I wish you had responded differently. I wish you would have said, "I want to be HAPPY." It's a simple and complicated answer. A person can change their mind or have a change of heart, but happiness is a state of being. You didn't know that your definition of happiness would change, as you changed and blossomed. Choosing a career for your life based on your knowledge as a 2nd grader might be a little presumptuous. Heck, choosing a career for your life at 33 years old, feels presumptuous!

Your life has had many changes, some have even reshaped your entire thought process. In your case, it changed for the better. As you finished your Master's Program, your only focus was becoming a Dean at a University. As you set out on this journey, you became laser focused on that goal. It wasn't until after a major life event, that your priorities shifted. You then realized that your mission in life was to pursue the heart of God. After you let go of your life's plan, you allowed God to lead you into a career that would fulfill His purpose. You quickly found out that your happiness was deeply rooted in your faith. The more you operated in your purpose, the happier you were with your life.

It's a scary journey. Like being suspended at the tippy top of a rollercoaster, scary! Being led by God when choosing a career is not common. Most people allow society to tell them that their career and faith have no correlation. I would have to respectfully disagree. If you knew then what you know now, you would have consulted God a long time ago. You would have prayed more in college, and consulted God before consulting an advisor. Perhaps you could have saved some money on student loans if you consulted God before you confirmed your plans. Regardless of how you get there, being happy, should be the goal. If it changes a few times along the way, that's okay too. Don't worry, BE HAPPY!

Jackie

A Mother's Love

BY MARIE WEATHERS

"Trust in the LORD with all thine heart; and lean not unto thine own understanding. In all thy ways acknowledge him, and he shall direct thy paths."

Proverbs 3:5-6

Your mother was your everything. You adored and loved her dearly. Although she passed away over 30 years ago, you continue to feel her presence. She was *your confidant, sister, friend, and your mother*. Momma was always there. Growing up, you felt a great deal of resentment. You lived in a basement apartment with rats as big as cats! Your three older brothers shared a room, and you had your own. Your mother was a hardworking woman. She was an incredible mother, and did the very best she could with what she had. She worked as a domestic worker for whites, cleaning and caring for their children and you resented her for that. You also resented her for leaving you alone so much while she worked. She was a single mother, and you never knew your father. Your brothers were older, and they were never home. Your mother worked countless hours to provide for you and your brothers. This left you to raise yourself. It was lonely being the only girl and the youngest.

You became pregnant at the age of 15 because of the lack of attention and love you felt at home. Your mother was ashamed that you got pregnant, so she sent you to live with your aunt in St. Louis. You didn't want to follow her rules, so your stay in St. Louis was short lived. When you returned home and had your first child, you got married to your child's father. Your mother signed for the marriage certificate, took you both to city hall, and you were a married woman. You had your first child at 15, married at 16, and 2nd child at 17 years old. Baby, your life was moving *FAST*! During this stage of your life, the relationship with your mother changed. The conversation was different. At 15 years old, you didn't know how to be a mother or a wife. You hardly knew who you were! Instead of your mother scolding you for the wrong decisions you made, she taught you how to be a mother. Your first marriage was short. It was a childhood marriage that only lasted 3 years.

After separating from your child's father, you had to learn how to care for your children on your own. You went back home to live with your mother to gain stability. You signed up for welfare, and took a class to become a patient care attendant. You finished the class, and found a job at St. Joseph Hospital. You rented your first apartment with pride. You finally felt a sense of independence, but you didn't have a clue of the challenges you would face as a single mother of two small children and working a full-time job. There were times you wouldn't be able to go to work because you didn't have anyone to care for the girls. They were still small and unable to stay home alone. Once, there was a snow storm and you had to work. You lived in a garden apartment. That snow was so high, you couldn't even see out of the windows. You had to call one of your older brothers over to shovel you out so you could go to work. The thing you feared most in that moment was being fired from the job that you desperately needed. As the girls became older, you began to leave them home alone. When things became really hard you sent them to live with your mother. Balancing motherhood and trying to grow up at the same time wasn't easy. You did some of the same things you resented your mother for. You were poor, and there were times the girls were raising themselves because you had to work. You didn't finish high school, so job options were few and they never paid much money. Like your mother, you did the best you knew how with what you had. There were even times you worked two jobs to make sure that the girls didn't go without.

You engaged in relationships thinking everyone you met was *the one*. By the time you were 36 years old, you had given birth to 5 girls. Five months after giving birth to your 4th child, you became pregnant with your 5th . During the pregnancy of your 4th child, you were in your 2nd marriage which was a very difficult relationship. Your mother became ill and passed away. The impact of her death was the greatest pain that you ever felt.

Your *confidant, sister, friend, and your mother* was gone. When things got hard, you would always go to her, but she was no longer there. It was difficult to process all the emotions that you felt. You lost yourself during that time. You needed your mother's love most after she was gone. You thought Momma would always be there. Over time, you began to understand that her words and love would last forever. One of her favorite bible verses was, *"Trust in the LORD with all thine heart; and lean not unto thine own understanding. In all thy ways acknowledge him, and he shall direct thy paths."*

At 75 years old, I have lived and learned many lessons along the way. One piece of advice I would give you is to hold on to your mother's favorite scripture. It's going to direct your path. Baby, let me tell you, no love is better than self-love. You gotta love yourself first. Forgive yourself for the things you regret, and focus on what you have instead of the things you don't. Balancing motherhood and trying to grow into the person you will become won't be easy, but you'll make it! Your strength and resilience are INCREDIBLE! Each one of your daughters will inherit it. You will provide them with all the resources they will need to succeed in life. Life will throw you some painful daggers, like the death of a child, but you will make it through! With each decade you will have lessons and opportunities, live and learn. Happiness is a choice, not a result of how life unfolds. Take advantage of traveling to different countries, it'll be an experience you will never forget. Never give up on true love. Don't look for it. It will find you. Time heals almost everything. Throw on that red lipstick, strut in those heels, and dance! Do what makes you happy.

Love Always,

Marie

Ticking Time Bomb

BY FELICIA HOUSTON

"Only I can change my life. No one can do it for me."

Carol Burnett

Dear Ticking Time Bomb,

Admit it. Life's not easy. Not as a kid, an adult, and definitely not easy for a teen. I see you in 8th grade struggling because certain kids are calling you the N-Word, and telling you to go back to Africa! Then, other kids are calling you nappy headed, wide nose, football head, and dry bones because you're so skinny. You're trying not to let it bother you, but some days you feel very overwhelmed. There will be days you won't want to fight, and other days you will fight because that's how you cope. You have to learn how to balance the stress of school, homework, friends, drama, and boys on your little shoulders. I bet you're wondering how you will cope with this busy life. You will figure it out. I promise, and you won't lose your mind.

I know you feel like your parents are judging every move you make, and you hate feeling like you're in prison. You can't go to sleep overs, you must be home before the street lights come on, and don't even think about going to any parties!

You've been grounded for months at a time. It sucks. It seems unreasonable, but your parents really do have your best interest at heart. Boundaries and rules are a sign of good parenting and tough love. You'll figure this out once you have kids of your own. Trust me.

As you start this high school adventure, please remember these few things:

1. Everyone will not like you, and that's okay. I know it's hard at thirteen, but you must always be YOU! If anyone has a problem with you, then maybe they're not worth keeping around. You and your feelings are important, and you should never settle for less.
2. Hold onto your faith no matter what it looks like. You are about to go to new places, but you belong there! #WeTrustGod
3. Spend time with your family. You're the oldest; your siblings will want to see you sometimes. Be present. They love you so

much for always protecting them; just don't forget about yourself.

4. You CAN do the impossible. It's a mindset. Get your mind right girl.

5. Sleep now, or it will affect you later in life. There is no such thing as a sleep bank! Lies!

6. Embrace your real & raw feelings, not just anger. You can't go through life fighting and dismissing people because they don't agree with you. Try to have an open mind. I know this is hard, but it's possible.

7. Learn to love your imperfections, and grow from your mistakes.

8. Remember, girls can be mean, boys can be cruel, and parents can seem intolerable, but the world is a beautiful place, and you are a beautiful girl!

Love you,

Be Selfish

BY ADEOLA POLLARD

"Sometimes I Forget Putting Myself First Isn't SELFISH But Necessary."

(Unknown)

Addie,

Every so often I wonder, "If I only knew then what I know now". You have such amazing qualities. You are a remarkable mother, daughter, sister, and more. The way you love and care for others, especially those that you love dearly is incredible. And your loyalty! Sometimes our best qualities will get in the way, your light will get dimmer, and you will lose direction on the goals you had for yourself. You will walk down a path where you become last to everything and everyone.

You dream of opening your own salon one day and you work diligently on plans. The floor plans look incredible, and your vision will stand out. Incorporating a children's area between the barbershop and beauty shop is a fabulous idea! After a few years of hard work, you finally saved the money to open. The reality of Kreations Salon & Barbershop was getting closer. You looked everywhere for the perfect space, but nothing seems to really catch your eye. You continue searching and finally stumble upon the space you've been looking for. After negotiations, the deal was not successful, and you are back to square one. As time passes, your dream of opening a salon seems further and further away. You decided to place Kreations on hold to invest into someone else's dream. This is someone you would give the world to. This is your biggest downfall! You will work so hard to help everyone around you accomplish their dreams. Although, this brought you so much joy and warmth, you will quickly see your dreams and goals fade away. As a result, Kreations never opened, and the investment you made for someone else never panned out.

That decision changed your path, and you started to tell yourself that your dreams didn't matter. You become a licensed cosmetologist, which was different from your original plan, but you will recognize your mistakes and make a new plan, a new dream!

My advice starts with telling you "BE SELFISH". Listen! Nothing is wrong with putting your goals and dreams at the forefront of your life. It will not stop you from being an awesome mom to your children, a great daughter, sister, or friend. Everyone else will be okay without your help, without giving all that's within. Being selfish isn't to slight anyone else and it doesn't mean you will never help anyone. It means you can work on you and accomplish your plans without guilt. It's knowing that you are doing what is best for you. Either people will support you or they won't. Either way it's OK!

Being Selfish will save you a lot of stress and unnecessary hardship. You may not see it now, but you are a POWERFUL, AMBITIOUS, HARDWORKING, INTELLIGENT, STRONG WOMAN!! You have so much to offer the world, and you will make a huge impact on so many.

Read this letter every time you feel you are getting off your path. YOU ARE IN CHARGE of your future, and putting yourself last will only delay your personal and professional successes. Remember you must love and care about you first. If you aren't together, you can't get anyone else together.

IT IS OKAY TO "BE SELFISH"!

Love You Dearly

Addie

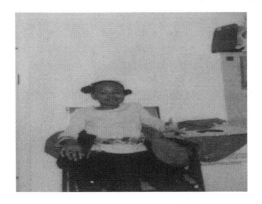

You Will Make it, Please Don't Give Up

BY JESSICA SOETAN- HOLT

"To be the best you must handle the worst."

(Unknown)

Dear Young Fly Jess,

You will make it, but don't you dare give up! I know it sucks right now; the trauma, the bullying, verbal and mental abuse. I bet you would never believe how your story changes. I know you hate to revisit this, but it's important for your healing. You have to understand that trauma, trouble, debt, and hurt will happen, but it will all be temporary, just please don't give up! Let's talk about the last 6 months of 8th grade. I want to take you back to the day Ms. Hicks told you, *"Lil girl the next time you are late for my class, you won't graduate from 8th grade, now get in here and sit on down".* You never told anyone what she said because you were too embarrassed to talk about what was going on at home. You were mortified, embarrassed, and ashamed that all your hard work was being threatened because of excessive tardiness.

Your grades were amazing. You pushed through, and even made the honor roll. Little did everyone around you know, every single night, you experienced trauma. Every single night, you were scared. Your guardian was a constant victim of domestic violence. You often hid the cordless phone under your pillow, just in case you had to call the police from the bathtub. She screamed in horror, **HELP ME! CALL THE POLICE JESSICA! PLEASE CALL THE POLICE!** After a while, the police stopped coming, but these haunting thoughts bombarded your mind; *"She's going to let him in again, he's going to bust down the door, someone is going to let him in the building, or he's going to be waiting for me in that piece of crap green car when I leave out for school."* You constantly overslept because of these fears. The continuous torture, the aftermath of disarray, and nightmares caused you to wake up late for school, having to run two long blocks. With all of this going on, guess what, you made it through. You prayed so much as a kid, don't ever forget the power of God. Jessica, you will make it through, but always remember, please don't give up.

I'm sure you want to know how to get through all this. Don't worry, I'll give you the spill. By the time you enter high school, you will develop a deep affection for writing. Your diary, journal, and note stash will be endless. Read them from time to time just to see how you were feeling, who you were crushing on, or who was bullying you. It will allow you to see how you have grown and also be a reminder that the things that upset you then, won't matter so much. Writing has been such a positive outlet for you. Writing brought you close to a person you hadn't seen in ten years. It'll help you through break ups. Writing has been such a therapeutic journey.

Fast-forward to the present, I've learned so much about being creative with words that I've created a personal brand and blog all on my own called: I'm Jess Sayin'. Find your outlet through the things that bring you joy and happiness. Even today, when I am feeling overwhelmed, I write a note to myself and state EXACTLY how I feel whether it's incompetent, unattractive, sad, stressed, happy, or blessed. I write it, read it out loud, fold it up, put it in my work bag, and go into prayer. The bible says *"Cast thy burden upon the Lord and he shall sustain thee: he shall never suffer the righteous to be moved"*- (Psalms 55:22) You see, I cast all my burdens down on paper, then I give it to the Lord. Once I've done that, I'll either throw the notes away because the negative energy or feelings have no space in my life, or I'll keep them as a reminder that God will provide as long as I do the work. Do the work Jess, don't give up.

As you venture out and make new memories, continue to use your words. Write down how you felt after pledging the most DIVASTATING Sorority, Delta Sigma Theta Sorority Inc. Use your words to describe the exhilarating feeling of finally showing off those pearly whites, brace free. Allow the paper to be your sounding board. This will prevent you from exploding with every emotion you've been trying to keep contained. Continue to make the world laugh with your words. Your writing will make you feel good. Write it out, until you cry it out. Stay prayerful. Your journaling will get you very far if you stay focused. Right now, you have such a hard exterior, but one day you'll be open to sharing your story and it will help others. Live the life you were meant to live. Write that book. Start those businesses. Secure the bag. Love on your husband, and make money together. Do it all because one day, it will all matter. I'm Jess Sayin, this book of life isn't even close to being completed. Just know you will make it, but please don't you dare give up.

With love,

Jess Sayin'

GUARD YOUR LOYALTY

BY RACHAEL N. TURNER

"Cease ye from man, whose breath is in his nostrils: for wherein is he to be accounted of."

Isaiah 2:22 (KJV)

Dear Young Rachael,

I am so proud of you! You are preparing to skip from 5th to 6th grade mid-year. You've made some great friends at your new school, and you see your future as limitless. Sometimes, I re-read your journal entry where you wrote your goals for 25-year-old us: Doctor, lawyer, married, and mother of twins living in New York. Your optimism will take you far.

You are extremely loyal, just like mom and dad, but not everyone will deserve multiple opportunities to experience your friendship. You are, by no means, obligated to tolerate anyone based on length of

77

relationship, the time you invested, nor the sincerity of their apology. Even those with the best intentions can still harm you. It doesn't make them a bad person, but you don't have to maintain that relationship.

At 23, you'll be promoted to manager of the entire banking department for a large investment company. There will be pressures caused by a merger that requires tedious processes, working with a remote team that doesn't understand nor respect the current processes, and the added pressure of being a female, the youngest, and only black manager at your location. Everyone will see how hard you work, and you will leave a great impression on many. Even leading to the promise of a future position. You will work so hard and push even when you don't feel like it. This will eventually burn you out and you'll want to quit. When you feel that urge to quit, don't ignore it. You will feel like you invested so much into your position. You like the work you do, but YOU are the most important part of the equation. They will be ok if you decide to leave. You were built to thrive regardless of your environment. YOU OWE THEM NOTHING! You owe it to yourself to keep moving forward and becoming the best YOU possible.

In any position or relationship, remember that no salary increase, profession of love, or gift should drown out the power of your intuition.

You will do anything for those that you love, and you want to fix everything! It's not your job to fix broken people. Remember that the greatest action you can take is prayer. Take all of the time you need to make a decision on the place that others have in your life. The one person you should be the most loyal to is God and yourself!

Love always!

Rachael

Mirror Mirror

BY STACEY C. WEATHERS

Love never gives up, never loses faith, is always hopeful, and endures through every circumstance.

1 Corinthians 13:7

The transition from kid to teenager was tough. You often think of the things that impacted you during this stage of your life. One of the most significant moments was starting High School in August of 1992. You were officially a teenager. No more of the little kid stuff, you were in the big leagues now. Your friends were all going to be there, but so were so many other students that you didn't know. Many of them were much bigger and older than you. You were happy and scared all at the same time because you didn't know what to expect. Countless thoughts were racing through your mind. "Would I get pushed into my locker? Would I get robbed of my lunch money like they do on T.V.?". Your emotions were all over the place. You wondered if people would like you, if you were smart enough, or even cute enough? You weren't sure how to express these thoughts to anyone, so you didn't.

80

I wish you heard how special you were, and that it didn't matter what anyone else thought. I wish you were told that the thoughts or feelings of others won't ever validate who you are. I wish your gifts and talents would have been noticed and nurtured. You were different from other kids your age, and at times it made you feel like an outcast. You always had a serious demeanor, but to them, you were trying to be grown. Grown? No! You were focused. What if the word "beautiful" was used to describe you, instead of funny looking, big lips, big nose, and nappy hair? Kids can be cruel, but so can adults. One particular day you stood in the mirror to see what others saw when they looked at you. What did they think was so ugly? Somewhere along the way, you started to believe what they said. It's so easy to believe the negative opinions of others especially when you don't have a strong foundation which is ultimately the responsibility of the adults who surround you.

As an adult, you will realize the things that filled your cup were toxic and distorted. Those things were not your TRUTH! Piece by piece you will destroy the LIES that tore you down inside for so many years. You will look in the mirror and affirm who you really are instead of affirming the thoughts of others. With each day you will confess with your mouth new thoughts. You become what you think, and what you think you will believe. You will realize your self-thoughts, positive or negative, will create your reality. The reality is *they* didn't see you properly. The same pieces that tore you down will be the bricks that build you up to reveal your strength. Brokenness will show you the depth of Stacey C. Weathers; beautiful inside and out, strong, worthy of all good things, loved and perfectly woven by God. *For you created my inmost being; you knit me together in my mother's womb. Psalms 139:13*

Stacey

Making it out Da Hood

BY REV DR CYNTHIA P. STEWART

"Blessed is she who has believed that the Lord would fulfill his promises to her."

Luke 1:45

You are from Chicago? You grew up in Englewood? Did you get shot at? Were you in a gang? Wait, how many degrees do you have? You said you are Dr. Cynthia Stewart? How did that happen? These are questions you've gotten over the years. Either in grad school, visiting other states, or meeting new people. Who knew that an African American little girl from the Southside of Chicago, who attended Catholic grammar and high school would make it out of "Da Hood". Well, you knew it because God put people in your life who saw your gifts and helped to develop them.

One key person, a Catholic priest, took you under his wing when you were in third grade. Now, let me paint a picture of you as a young girl. You are the youngest of three children, and the only girl. You grew up with a single mother, who was on government assistance because she could no longer work due to an illness. You didn't know your father. This caused you to be an angry little girl, who expressed that pain through fighting. Every Monday in grammar school you went skating. You loved to skate because it took away from being concerned about your mother's illness, and whether she would die on you one day. Yes, you loved skating, but you also loved to fight. There wasn't one Monday when you didn't push or punch someone. Many times, it was for no reason at all except, they looked at you funny, they may have said something you did not like, or you just didn't like them. Well, the Priest noticed this pattern and pulled you to the side. He wanted to know why you were filled with all this anger. At the time, you didn't have a reason for him. As you got older, you came to understand the root cause. You were a scared little girl, who was unsure of who she was and why she was called to be on this earth. The Priest saved your life. He allowed you to work alongside him at the rectory and school gym. He saw the gift of service and the passion to help others in you. Education and service became your means of escape from life's challenges.

Even though you grew up in an impoverished community in Chicago (Englewood), you broke the stereotypes that society places on African American youth from single-parent, low-income households. Your

Catholic school education and faith provided you with the spiritual foundation that helped to form a spiritual identity as a child of God. This foundation included recognizing your calling in ministry at an early age, which allowed you to plan and implement spiritual retreats for your peers while you were a teenager. This continued into your adult life. Yes, you broke the stereotype of having a child out of wedlock, being addicted to drugs, not completing high school, or even getting killed before you turned 21. Well, let me encourage you. You will have three master's degrees and a Doctor of Philosophy degree. You will have the opportunity to teach in higher education for several years. You will be blessed to travel out of the country countless times. You will also mentor over 1,000 teenagers through spiritual retreats. Your path will lead you to the classes of Ivy League universities. So, don't let anyone tell you, you cannot make it out of the "Da Hood". Because you can. All you need is someone like my Priest to see your gifts and help you unfold your greatness. There is a genius inside of all of us, we just need the people God places in our lives to help us see it, develop it, and live it out. Who has God placed in your life? Make sure not to reject them, but accept them because you will see their value when you get older.

I am blessed to say that into your adult life, you continued the relationship with your Priest up until his death six years ago. He became the father you didn't have. He taught you how to deal with many life lessons, and how to have a relationship with God. You would not be the woman you are today, if he didn't come into your life and save you from being that angry little girl who hurt others because she was hurting. Now, you like to help others, the way he helped you.

Cynthia P. Stewart, PhD

What's Extra?

BY TOT JONES

"Those who sow in tears will reap with songs of joy."

Psalm 126:5

Dear Tot,

One definition of the word "*extra*" reads: To a greater extent than usual; especially. Synonyms for the word "*extra*" are exceptionally, particularly, amazingly, outstandingly, and extremely. Everyone wanted to know why you were so "*extra*". They'll eventually have a front row seat to the answer. I know right now you are not convinced that you are "*extra*". You're 17 years old, and "*extra*" is your normal. But my love, you are "*extra*" indeed, in every sense of the word.

It's senior picture day and everyone is in their classy picture day attire. Here you are in GUCCI pants! Seriously, GUCCI print pants? This moment set you apart. Your peers accepted you. It was noted that Tot is just EXTRA! Everyone got it, but you! You must dive into God's purpose for this extra-ness!

You have many questions twirling in your mind. "Will I be successful? Will I go to college?" So many questions, yet no clarity. Just know, you will be okay. Everything happening to you is for your good. Don't be discouraged, be ENCOURAGED. You will experience more pain than you think you can handle, but it is all a part of God's plan for your life. Your secret ingredient to healing is Jesus Christ. Men won't heal the pain my love, only Jesus. There will come a time where you will shut down your creativity for a paycheck. The money is good, but your growth will be stunted. KEEP WRITING! Keep an outlet for your thoughts. It's the thing that sets you apart, and you must not let anyone tell you differently.

10 things you must know:

1.   God loves you so much.

2.   Life is not unfair. You are being developed. Your story is being written.

3.   FOCUS Tatiana! Boys will be there, trust me. Focus on your future.

4.   You are going to regret not going away to college! GO!!

5.   You are way more creative than you realize.

7.   When you move out it's going to hurt your brother. Open your eyes to how he feels.

8.   Learn to budget, NOW!

9. Your love for clothes is different...keep an eye on that fashion thing.

10. You will have JOY!

Your journey is pretty eventful...document the whole thing. Embrace your extra and whatever you do, do not suffer in silence. God has created you to be *exceptionally* bold, *particularly* different, *amazingly* creative, *outstandingly* courageous, and *extremely* blessed.

Totally Tot

I May Bend but I'll Never Break!

BY LORI T. GRUMBACH

"Real integrity is doing the right thing, knowing that nobody's going to know whether you did it or not."

Oprah Winfrey

Dear Lori,

I know you hear that you're beautiful so often throughout the day, pretty much EVERY DAY! I also know that when you look in the mirror, beauty is the last thing you see. 19 years old, in a new city, miles away from home and eager to accomplish so many goals. Meeting the wrong young man delayed all of your dreams! It is now crystal clear that the words that constantly rang through your ears were much more damaging than the punches that touched your skin. You found your spirit broken, and you were on the verge of death begging for your life. Your life has drastically changed from being the upbeat life of the party, to becoming this lifeless spirit that walked around ashamed of what had transpired in your life.

So many scars are hidden on the inside. When those scars are revealed, you will be able to undoubtedly see your beauty. You have been beaten, either mentally or physically, by every man that you've ever loved. You will be mistreated so much, the concept of trust will be erased from your heart. Lori, don't believe the harsh words that have been said to you – over and over and over again! Stop believing that you aren't good enough for the cowards that can't be honest and loving. Push past the pain, and walk into your purpose.

Take control of your emotions or you will become a bitter woman, lashing out at anyone you encounter. This will stifle your success. Choose love through all things. Love yourself first, so you don't have to compete for the acceptance of others. Otherwise, you will be misunderstood and the greatness that lives in you will never be shown to the world. The fight against yourself will hold you back from completing your goals. Embrace who you are, ALL that you are, and others will accept you.

Lori, I want you to know that you ARE beautiful, but you are so much more than beauty. You have so much to share with the world, don't hold it inside! Talk often, talk loudly, and share your story. Other young women will hear your cries and know that they are not alone. Once you release your pain, you'll be able to smile sincerely each day of your life. Joy will reside so deeply in your heart, nothing or no one will be able to take it away.

Sending lots of love and hugs,

Lori Tamara

...But God

BY DONNA M. MANTECA

All these blessings will come unto you and accompany you if you obey the Lord your God.

Deuteronomy 28:2

My Dear Donna, it is your senior year of high school. Prom, graduation, college, dorm life, and most of all, freedom! Donna, I am so excited for you. School hasn't always been easy like it is for your sisters, but you made it. All those nights praying and studying before tests, have truly been worth it. Life has been good these past 16 years, in spite of the normal ups and downs of growing up.

Deuteronomy 28:2 All these blessings will come unto you and accompany you if you obey the Lord your God.

Although your senior year brought excitement, it also came with unexpected change. I know you think your world has fallen apart, and

93

you are questioning God right now. I hear your cries: "Lord why have you allowed this illness to fall upon me? What have I done to deserve Lupus? Will I live, or will this thing kill me before I even get a chance to live? Why me Lord? Why me? I confess all that I have done, and I will turn away from all sin if you just make it go away! I am so scared Lord."

Philippians 4:6 Do not be anxious about anything, but in every situation by prayer and petition, with thanksgiving, present your requests to God.

Donna, I want you to know that pain, fear, and heartache will happen in your life. It may be self-inflicted or caused by some outside situation which you have no control. You will question your faith, and all that God has done for you. You will forget what you have learned and experienced. You will feel defeated by yet another test. I want you to know that your test will be your testimony, and your fears will strengthen your faith.

Lupus allowed you to receive a scholarship to college from the Department of Rehabilitation. You became a mentor to other young people who have been diagnosed with Lupus. You established a health club for youth with physical and medical disabilities. You treat your body as a temple and representation of what God can do.

As you go through things in life, it will allow you to speak from what you know to be true. Those around you will believe you, and therefore believe in God who said, "I will never leave you or forsake you." Deuteronomy 31:6.

You will have pain and heart ache, "but God" said cast all your anxiety upon Him. You will be afraid, "but God" said fear not for I am with you always.

Donna

Strength Doesn't Have to be Loud

BY CANDICE PAYNE

"I fall somewhere on the spectrum between Provers 31 and Tupac."

(Unknown)

One of your greatest challenges was choosing your battles during your high school years. You may not have shown up planning to fight, but you wouldn't back down either. If someone threw an insult your way, you had a swift one to throw right back. Most of the time, yours were aimed to shut it down. You wouldn't even spend much time trying to conjure it up. Clapping back was a skill. If a person had wronged you or someone you loved, you were going to make it known. Brush it off. It's just words, right? Nope, CONFRONT! You believed being passive made you weak, and you should never let anyone get over on you. Over the years, you've grown to have a greater appreciation for the word meek. You used to view the word as being spineless, and didn't realize the need for the humility it required.

This might be kind of lame to some, but The Lion King is one of your favorite movies. Let's focus on Sarabi's character (Simba's Mom). She was the queen of Pride Rock, and clearly a woman of strength. Towards the end of the movie, Scar called out to her concerning the lack of food. While she walked past the hyenas, they were growling, barking, and snarling at her as if they were trying to intimidate her. Sarabi walked past them confidently with her head held high. She didn't bother to look or make eye contact with the hyenas because they were beneath her. She's a queen, they ate her scraps. Sometimes the best clap back is your silence. Accusations will come, and sometimes it will be hard to fight the urge to fight back, especially when the words they speak are untrue. Learn to walk past your enemies with your head held high. You finally understand that the power you have within you could expose the insecurities of others around you, including those in authority. However, humility has been an important character trait, and it has taken time to develop over the years. Always remember, (Like Sarabi) you are a brave, strong, and powerful young lady. If you wanted to, you could rip them to shreds with your words in response to their attacks, but hostility is beneath you and causes you to stoop down to their level. Stay Humble! It's a necessary strength!

Candice

God's Plan

BY FRANCIS MARIE CASH

"Blessed are the pure in heart, for they will see God."

Matthew 5:8

The decade of 1940 brought everything you every wanted. You attended Kentucky State University and received your Bachelor's Degree in Social Work; later earning a Master's Degree. Kentucky State University was a college designed for people of color. There, you gained independence and began to live the life you dreamed of as a little girl from St. Louis. You would become the first in your family to attend college. You had three dreams for your life; Go to college, get married and start a family and work in the field of Social Work. Back then, girls graduated from high school, got married, and started a family. Many worked as domestic servants or in factories. You were determined to be a black girl who was college educated!

After completing your degree at Kentucky State University, you went to Chicago to begin your career in Social Work, later becoming supervisor over your department. During that time, you met the love of your life who was a serviceman. He was everything you dreamed of for a husband. One of the happiest moments of your life was when you became pregnant because you always wanted a family. Not long after becoming pregnant you had a miscarriage. It was devastating! Even more heartbreaking, you learned that you would no longer be able to conceive children. That news changed everything you thought your life would be. It was a very difficult time in your relationship. He couldn't bare not being able to have children and neither could you. The two of you experienced a rollercoaster of emotion and soon drifted apart. It was a very painful and disappointing time. You often questioned why God would allow such a terrible thing to happen to you. God doesn't make mistakes. We never understand why in the moment and sometimes we never quite understand. Eventually, love found you again. He wasn't the love of your life, but you loved him dearly.

You never became a mother in the biological sense of the word, but you were blessed to be a mother figure to many single mothers over the course of 38 years in the field of Social Work. You helped single mothers gain skills to become employed and support their families. You were tough. You had to be. They needed to know that life wasn't going to be easy, but it was going to be worth it. In the midst of that toughness, you also showed them love. Showing them that tough love ultimately taught them how to love themselves. In 1984, you retired. After retirement, many of the women you worked with over the years kept in touch with you. That was a testament of the difference you made in their lives. Although you still mourn never having any children of your own, God blessed your life with spiritual daughters. HE also allowed you to help care for your adopted brother. Your mother adopted him when she was in her 60's. His mother was unable to care for him, so she brought him home as a newborn. You loved him from the moment you laid eyes on him. He had beautiful dark skin, and a head of shiny thick curly hair. As your mother began to age, she was no longer able to care for him. At that time, you were in the height of your career, so you and your aunt took care of him. You loved him dearly and spent a great deal of time with him. He passed away 4 years ago, at the age of 53.

Now, I'm going to be honest with you. I was hesitant to write this letter, but there are some lessons I've learned in my 95 years on this earth that I know you would want to know. Marie, let me tell you, a joyful life doesn't mean you have the life you planned. God's plans are always better than ours. That's one of the most important lessons you will learn in your lifetime. Life becomes complicated when we aren't able to let go of our plans and embrace the plans that God has for our life. There was a quote that I once read, "You want to make God laugh, tell him about your plans."

As a young woman you worked hard, and you were so determined. Working hard and being determined is a good thing, but don't allow it to consume you. You wanted to succeed in life and you wanted the same for everyone around you. At some point, you have to let people take care of themselves. Your grandmother used to tell you to allow people to handle their own business. As you mature, you will understand that allowing people to handle their own business meant keeping your peace of mind and making room for the things that you enjoy. At 95 years old, I'm giving you the same advice young Marie. Go to church every Sunday, take care of yourself, and do all the things you enjoy. Spend time with the people you love because they won't always be around. Take it from somebody who has lived a long life.

Francis *Marie* Cash

Broken Crayons Still Color

BY YANNI BROWN

"BROKEN Crayons still color boldly, in and outside of the lines while making beyoutiful rainbows!"

(Unknown)

Oh, if I just had a moment to speak to you when you were just beginning to feel. Feelings that you didn't understand, feelings that you didn't even know you had. There are so many things that I would share to help you heal. It would be beautiful to look into your eyes and let you know that broken crayons still color! Life is going to come at you fast, flip your world upside down, and dangle you back and forth. HOLD ON!

You were thirteen and in love. There was no question about it! He was the one. The one that you had decided to give your virginity to. In your mind, it was the fairytale that young girls create; the princess and her prince charming. The moment was perfect. You were in love and he was simply in like. The moment came and went like a thief in the night, and you were left with the residue of that moment. The fairytale had ended, and there was certainly no" happily ever after". Shortly after, and I do mean shortly, you broke up and just like that he was on to the next. I want you to know that "Sean" is not the last guy you will ever love! It is okay to love because love is a gift. You have no control over what others do with that amazing gift.

This experience changed your life, although you didn't know how until years later. You thought you were emotionally ready for this intimate moment. Since you weren't, it completely changed your perception of love and everything you thought it was. The fact that he chose someone else, after you gave him the best part of you, affected how you looked for love. It was mostly in all of the wrong places. The love for yourself was lost in the midst of giving him all your love. So, for many years your self-love was defined in pleasing others. As you grow into your womanhood, you've learned to love yourself.

In the moments when you are unsure and insecure, remember these words. Listen to your instincts, they will protect you from things seen and unseen. If you let it, your instincts will protect you from the outline of blackness that can shape who you will become. You can BE anything you want to be. Don't let love, life, anyone, or anything tell you differently. While I know you would rather create, it will be so very important for your future to have something to fall back on, when your cup is empty.

Baby girl, your giving spirit will draw others to you; always wanting to sip from your cup. Your energy commands it. Please know that you cannot pour from an empty cup. So, gather those who can and will restore and pour back into you with rich, bold, and beautiful colors.

Last, but certainly not least remember that broken crayons do color! It is because they are broken that they will blend together to make the most beautiful picture of life. Only you can create that. Who you are will always be deeply rooted in who you were, the things you will go through, and the journeys that will take you there. ENJOY them all; the good, the bad and the ugly. Don't be so hard on yourself. Learn from them, let them shape you, hold you, mold you, caress you, and make you better. That's what life is all about. Amazing experiences that allow you to be exactly who God intended you to be.

Yanni Brown

The Promise

BY KELLE HOLMES

"Your word is a lamp for my feet, a light on my path."

Psalm 119:105 NIV

Dear Kelle,

You have what it takes to be successful in whatever path you choose. The first step is for you to believe in yourself. You have hopes and dreams of becoming a doctor. You go through all the steps that lead to the path of medical school. In high school, you received good grades in order to get scholarships to afford college. You want to go to a renowned university, preferably one with a medical school. God's grace, along with your hard work and commitment, gets you accepted to Loyola University. You were so excited because not only is Loyola a medical school, but there is a hospital you can work in when you graduate. The classes you are taking are for pre-medicine majors. "Keep your eyes on the prize" is what your mother always said.

You were introduced to a program which helped minorities who were interested in the medical field. The Chicago Area Health and Medical Careers program was affiliated with different hospitals which allowed you to get exposure with patients. You volunteered at Provident Hospital in the emergency room and also at the University of Chicago Children's Hospital. The program paid for you to take both Kaplan and Princeton review test preparation courses in order to get you ready for the big medical exam. Free tutoring was offered if needed. You had so many resources. You studied abroad in Spain. There is no excuse not to achieve this awesome goal. So, what happened to 20 year old Kelle becoming a doctor?

You started doubting yourself. You became fearful of not being successful, fear of the unknown. There was a voice in the background telling you that you couldn't be a doctor. You couldn't get higher than a 'C' in science. You didn't pass the practice MCAT, how do you think you'll ever pass the real one? At this point you feel like a failure. You have not only let yourself down, but your parents and family who have been cheering you on and believing in you. Everyone has been waiting for the big moment and it never came. You allowed the voice of the enemy to defeat you.

During that season of fear, you learned that maybe God's plan was different than yours. As you smiled through the tears and frustration, God continued speaking to you. You graduated from Loyola University with a Bachelor of Arts degree in Spanish after four years of rigorous studying. You may not have gone to medical school, but you followed your ultimate dream of inspiring others to live healthier lives. As an Integrative Nutrition Health Coach, you educate others through group and one on one coaching at churches, schools, and in community settings. You will find a great level of joy in empowering others to make health changes which are the cornerstones of living longer and healthier lives.

Be open, and ready for change when God redirects your path. His promises are *always* true. Hold on to the promise that what God has for you is for you. Be obedient and allow him to direct your path. You will never be lead in the wrong direction. *"What no eye has seen, what no ear has heard, and what no human mind has conceived" -- the things God has prepared for those who love him—1 Corinthians 2:9* You must change the way you think and catch yourself when your mind tells you what you cannot do. With a thankful heart offer up your prayers and requests to God. Then, because you belong to Christ Jesus, God will bless you with peace that no one can completely understand. And this peace will control the way you think and feel.

Sincerely,

Kelle

The Good Life

BY DR NGONZI CRUSHSHON

"A person's most useful asset is not a head full of knowledge, but a heart full of love, an ear ready to listen and a hand willing to help others."

(Unknown)

Dear Ngonzi,

As a young girl, you felt self-conscious about your body and self-esteem, but you are beautiful from the inside out. Recognize that beauty is not just your skin tone, acne bumps, or the size of your hips or lips. Beauty comes from within. It is who you believe you are, and you have so much more to offer the world than your looks. There is nothing wrong with you. God made you exactly the way He wanted.

Society will try to paint a picture of how your life should look, they call it "The Good Life". Don't believe this twisted message. You will learn that "The Good Life" does not look like the fairytale or picture you have in your mind. It's what you make it. It's a simple concept, with lots of hard work involved. You will realize it isn't the external factors that matter. It is the inward journey that matters most. It's how you treat people. It's making time to connect with others on a soul level. When you live in the moment and walk in your purpose, you are living "The Good Life". With time you have the opportunity to elevate higher and higher. You will renew your mind and utilize different perspectives from people of all walks of life. This may not make sense to you now, but it will become clearer as you experience life.

Your life didn't look like the lives of other children. While your friends were hanging out and partying, you were being molded to walk in your destiny. You volunteered in church, were homeschooled, played an instrument, and kept distractions to a minimum. You often wondered why your life couldn't be "regular" like the other kids. You had no idea all these things were preparing you for your purpose. There will be moments where you will be fearful to move on to the next step in your life's journey. You will question if you even have the "goods" to make it. Rest in knowing that you will make it. You'll make it through college, careers, relationships, and multiple losses. Your ministry will change, touch, and heal many people's lives. Don't let the fear of the unknown block your path. As you mature, you will continue to have fears, but you are learning to stare fear right in the face. You are learning that when you fall, you do not fail. You get up and keep trying.

This world is yours, and you can achieve whatever you can conceive. Think outside the box, and don't let others limit you. You can write the book, be an international speaker, have four or more careers; a psychologist, Neuropsychology professor, best-selling author, and real estate agent. Just stay in communion with God. Pray, meditate, and learn who you are culturally and spiritually.

I love you for who you are on the inside, your good heart and giving spirit. Stick to your goals, morals, and values without stepping on others to get to the "top". You have great things ahead of you. There is enough success and wealth for everyone.

Ngonzi Truth Crushshon, Psy.D.

Bloom Where You are Planted

BY ARCHANA LIGGINS

"For I know the plans I have for you," declares the LORD, "plans to prosper you and not to harm you, plans to give you hope and a future."

Jeremiah 29:11

Archana,

I'm writing from your future to make you aware of a few things that will be life-changing lessons! The growing pains, lessons learned, and the memories you create growing up will not be forgotten. They'll be considered wisdom and knowledge as you mature. Girl, God is going to use you at an early age. God is directing your path. It looks like a maze because your life didn't go by your written plan, it's going to go by His! The rap you wrote about your career path and life plan after 8th grade will be null and void soon after high school graduation. It went a little something like this; "1991, I'll be on my way to high school not being a fool and staying in school. 1995 is going to fly by and off to

111

college I go! But wait there's more, Y2K is going to bring more, cuz Imma get a master's degree to get that mo-ney! And something about you being all that…". Little did you know, your plan was thwarted by God's greater plan for your life. Archana, buckle your seatbelt because you are about to go on the ride of your life. As your future husband will always say, it does get "Greater Later".

Friendliness is a natural characteristic of yours. Just because you are nice and cordial, doesn't mean that everyone is going to like you. The truth is, by 7th grade you will learn a huge lesson on characteristics. You exhibited characteristics of love and cheerfulness, while your classmates showed themselves to be rude and disrespectful. I'm glad you had self -control and didn't get the grammar school blues. You didn't let your classmates hold you back or discourage you. Keep going to school, and ignore the "Ar- Ar-ArchieBall" chants and the horse noises. Your teeth are big and well kept. The taunting is going to hurt your feelings, but you'll later realize kids are cruel. These cruel words will become distant whispers in the wind after you begin to ignore them. I'm proud of you for grinning and bearing that time of your life.

As a young person, you can have fun but don't be a follower. Your friends will later say, "You were always doing something different" and "You stayed in your own lane". There is something greater in you, waiting to be birthed. That nudge to do right is discernment at an early age. You want to be a leader, but you also wanted to be liked. That tug and pull is hard to manage at a young age. You may not understand it, but being a leader requires you to be mindful of what you say and do. These things can affect your future. You aren't a "goodie two shoes", you just know in your heart what is right and what is wrong. You don't get this from your pastor or your parents. You know because God said so! He will send you reminders, and as you have always believed, "When prayers go up…blessings come down". Keep praying, "I just want to do right, God in your name, Amen!"

I can do all this through him who gives me strength. Philippians 4:13

I don't think you will realize until years later that you were a teenage entrepreneur. Nails by Chana, a 16-year-old licensed nail technician, specializing in nail designs and nail extensions! Yes, working in a salon after school was an experience that helped you build people skills to use later in life. Your first official job was working for yourself. You learned a lot about yourself and others; the good, bad and ugly! When you get older, you will reflect on those days because they will be filled with so much significance. Building relationships and communication is a part of life. By this time in your life, you were grooming more than nails, you were grooming more positive characteristics. You were building loyalty with your clients and operating in excellence to become a successful nail technician. You trusted the process at an early age and I thank you for it, "God never gives you more, than you can handle." Keep building relationships because your networking will pay off later in life.

And we know that in all things God works for the good of those who love him, who have been called according to his purpose. Romans 8:28

Archana, I advise you to stay in your lane, do things differently, and trust God in all that you do. You never want to be in anybody else's lane. Trust me, as you grow, you will understand why your lane is where you belong. Celebrate and recognize your successes, big or small. Your life's experiences will shape you, and your lane will be an important part of your life. You will trail blaze in that lane. You will also set new standards because you have what it takes. You will prove yourself to the girl who becomes a woman in the mirror. You only want to be the best version of that woman. She is educated, she has knowledge, her smile is beautiful, her network is large, her personality and drive are infectious. Her love for God is grander, her love for her family is immeasurable. Her potential is limitless, and her experiences will continue to shape her to do better and be better. You will be proud of yourself, even though your life didn't go as planned. You trusted God, and went on His journey!

I love you AP,
Best Wishes Forever, AL

SIXTEEN

BY LASHONDA MOORE

"If you can't fly, run; if you can't run, walk; if you can't walk, crawl; but by all means keep moving."

Dr. Martin Luther King

Dear LaShonda,

This letter is filled with pearls of wisdom, as you make your way along life's exciting, tumultuous, and adventurous highways. It's important to note that there will be good days and unfortunately challenging days, but as long as you learn the lessons that life brings you – taking one day at a time – you will be just fine. Understand that when you don't like the world the way it is; change it – as it starts with you. Maintain a balance with everything. Ultimately, love yourself and your love will permeate as it's contagious to others that you encounter. Remember that God is love and forgives us on a continual basis as He knows your heart.

"And be ye kind, one to another, tenderhearted, forgiving one another, even as God in Christ forgave you." (Ephesians 4:32 - NKJV) This is a scripture that you learned at the tender age of six. You will keep it in the forefront of your mind as challenges come your way. You were always a happy child, having a heart to help others. Although your childhood was met with some very painful events, you still maintained and continued to persevere, living a fulfilling life. Growing up in the inner city allowed you to see and learn a great deal. Wisdom and humility has come from some of those experiences. On a more intimate note, at age 16, you had an abortion with a guy you lost your virginity to. This changed the trajectory of your life. You were confused, hurt, and mixed with all sorts of emotions. In your mid-twenties, you will grow spiritually and ask God for his forgiveness. You will be at peace, and gain comfort in knowing that He forgave you and in turn, forgive yourself. Consequently, you will share your journey with your daughters and other young ladies – being an encouragement for them to love themselves and most importantly, that God's love supersedes all.

LaShonda

Use Your Wings Girl!

TIFFANY M. FINCHER

"Turn your wounds into wisdom."

-Oprah

Dear Sandy Brown-Haired Girl,

In the photo, you were sitting outside the townhouse, where you lived in the early years of your life. You were sucking your thumb as you often did to find comfort. Looking into your eyes, I can see the sadness, confusion, and worry. I remember this time period very vividly. You were about 4 or 5 years old when everything began to change. You were present physically, but mentally in another world. One particular day, you were sitting in an empty classroom at school. Everyone had gone outside for recess. You stayed in to make up class work and receive help with an assignment. In that moment, you weren't doing either. Instead, you stared out the window daydreaming, as you watched your classmates play. You weren't the highest achieving student in school because you were simply trying to figure out everything that was happening in your life. Teachers were concerned because you were guarded and withdrawn. I wonder if they knew the pain you felt from missing your mother? After your parents divorced, you and your sister lived with Daddy. You didn't understand "Grown up stuff", and you certainly didn't know how to articulate your feelings. So, your coping mechanism was to shut down. You and your sister were asked who you wanted to live with. I only 5 years old being asked to make a grown-up choice. Throughout the years, when things become harder, you will continue to shut down. If you didn't talk about it maybe it wouldn't hurt so bad.

It wasn't until you were 8 years old that you began to come out of your shell. By then, you moved into a new neighborhood, and started at a new school. You began to embrace the idea of socializing with your peers. When you were 13 years old, your father remarried. Every Sunday for months, your step-mother would take you, your sister, and your step brother to visit churches in hopes of finding a church home. Every Sunday you dreaded visiting yet another church and sitting through another service. Your sister loved it! She even had a bible of her own. One Sunday you visited, "New Christian Valley" now known as "Valley Kingdom Ministries International". *YOU HAD NEVER EXPERIENCED WORSHIP LIKE THAT!* When they asked guests who were looking for a church home to stand, all of you stood. That moment changed your life *FOREVER*! You would go every Sunday. Sure, you had been to church before, but that's just it. You had been to church. You never experienced a relationship with God. Developing the relationship changed everything. You didn't realize it then, but that special connection with HIM would help you discover the *wings* you didn't know you had.

If there is anything I would have told you throughout your childhood and young adult years, I would say, don't worry so much. Stop being so hard on yourself. Tiff, perfection is overrated, trust me! Be patient and give yourself permission to feel *all of your emotions.* Silencing how you feel will only hurt you. Always be graceful, but when you don't like something, say it. If someone offends, you let them know. Acknowledging how you feel will be uncomfortable, but the truth that it holds is where your power lies.

Open your heart and forgive your mother, it's necessary. Seek understanding, it's necessary. The blessings that will manifest from both forgiveness and understanding will blow your mind! As much as you tell yourself you are fine with the way things have been, you're lying to yourself. You need her as much as she needs you. Tell her how you feel. It is never too late to have a healthy relationship with her. Fight for it! You can start right where you are.

I would also tell you to quiet the noise. In a society that teaches you that you aren't productive if you aren't moving know that it is okay to be still. Movement doesn't always mean progress. Those moments of stillness are when your soul speaks. It is there that you find true direction, authenticity and truth. Be still and listen.

You will face storms in your life. Some of the storms might feel like they will never end. Those storms will change you. They will reveal who you are, and what you are made of. In those moments, God will use you as you doubt yourself. He will use you when you are **SCARED TO DEATH**, and when you are so nervous that it makes you sick to your stomach. It won't be pretty, but know that it isn't about you. He is doing something big*!* As you push through each obstacle that life throws your way face each of them with a spirit of gratitude. Give thanks in advance....

Everything that you experience will serve a significant purpose. It will shape you into the person that you will eventually become. The confusion will be a road map that will lead you to your passion for working with youth and families. The sadness and worry will manifest into strength. You will find the courage to use your voice. Be brave enough to listen to your heart and strong enough to live your purpose. *Use your wings girl!*

The last thing I would tell you is that once you discover your wings don't be afraid to use them. You will find undeniable power that will make you UNSTOPPABLE! Own it! Walk in It! Talk in It! Live your destiny with Your Own Style and *Grace*! You have been created with purpose!

Fly sandy brown-haired girl! *Use your wings!*

Tiffany Marie

Grace

KEYS TO GRACE

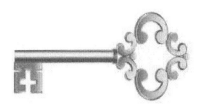

Keys to Grace

BY TIFFANY M. FINCHER

Keys to Grace is a short devotional to read over the course of 12 weeks. Read one devotional per week starting on Sunday. Each *key* includes a weekly goal, prayer and reflection. At the end of each week take a few minutes to reflect on the prior week.

Invite friends and family to join you in your weekly prayer, talk about your reflections and pray for each other.

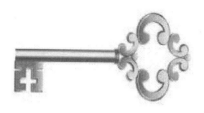

GRACE

Do something kind for someone who has hurt you. It will not be easy, but DO IT!

Say this Prayer

Father, Help to heal the hurt that _____ has caused and help me to see _____ as you do.

Amen

Reflection

_____

_____

_____

_____

_____

_____

_____

_____

_____

_____

_____

_____

_____

_____

_____

_____

_____

_____

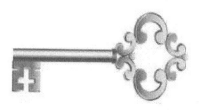

GRACE

During your prayer time, sit in silence. Listen to hear God's voice speak to you.

Say this Prayer

God, help me rest in you.

Amen

Reflection

_____

_____

_____

_____

_____

_____

_____

_____

_____

_____

_____

_____

_____

_____

_____

_____

_____

GRACE

Pray over broken relationships. Pray that God's will is done whether that is to reconcile or to establish closure.

Say this Prayer

God, Help me give grace and love toward

_____. Soften my heart toward _____ and

theirs toward me.

Amen

Reflection

_____

_____

_____

_____

_____

_____

_____

_____

_____

_____

_____

_____

_____

_____

_____

_____

_____

_____

GRACE

Take five minutes out of each day this week to share your anxieties and fears with God. Be honest. Prayer with Him is a no judgement zone. He hears your words and your heart.

Say this Prayer

God, Thank you in advance for transforming my deepest fears into courage for the sake of giving you glory.

Amen

Reflection

_____

_____

_____

_____

_____

_____

_____

_____

_____

_____

_____

_____

_____

_____

_____

_____

_____

_____

_____

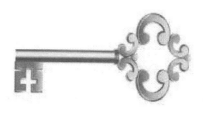

GRACE

Reflect on a time when you felt loved the most. Give that kind of love to someone in your life who you know really needs it most.

Say this Prayer

God, Help me to make time in my life to pour love into others.

Amen

Reflection

_____

_____

_____

_____

_____

_____

_____

_____

_____

_____

_____

_____

_____

_____

_____

_____

_____

_____

GRACE

It can be difficult to believe in the things that we cannot see or understand. In this season, what are you struggling to trust God with? *Pray that you will have increased confidence in God's power.*

Say this Prayer

God, I trust you. I trust that you are powerful and have the ability to work things out for my good.

Amen

Reflection

_____

_____

_____

_____

_____

_____

_____

_____

_____

_____

_____

_____

_____

_____

_____

_____

_____

_____

GRACE

What is something God has been telling you to do, but you have put it off? Get started before this week is over.

Say this Prayer

God, Give me the courage to act on the assignment that you have given me. Help me to know that if you have provided the vision you will provide every provision needed to carry out your vision.

Amen

Reflection

_____

_____

_____

_____

_____

_____

_____

_____

_____

_____

_____

_____

_____

_____

_____

_____

_____

GRACE

In today's society developing friendships is not what it used to be. Pick up the phone and schedule a lunch or dinner with a friend. Make the time to develop deeper and more meaningful relationships.

Say this Prayer

God, Reveal the people you want me to journey

through life with.

Amen

Reflection

_____

_____

_____

_____

_____

_____

_____

_____

_____

_____

_____

_____

_____

_____

_____

_____

_____

GRACE

Write down your *BIGGEST* and *BOLDEST* prayer.
One that you have been too afraid to pray for out
loud. Write it down and place it on your mirror.
Look in the mirror and pray this prayer out loud
every day for 7 days. Start TODAY!

Say this Prayer

God, Give me the courage to be consistent and

confident in praying my BIGGEST AND BOLDEST

prayers.

Amen

Reflection

_____

_____

_____

_____

_____

_____

_____

_____

_____

_____

_____

_____

_____

_____

_____

_____

_____

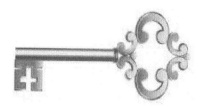

GRACE

How has God used some of life's most difficult seasons to transform you into the person you are today?

Say this Prayer

God, help me to remember the warranty of grace that you have granted over my life. My trails will continue to develop me and show me my strength.

Amen

Reflection

_____

_____

_____

_____

_____

_____

_____

_____

_____

_____

_____

_____

_____

_____

_____

_____

GRACE

Create a list of things in your life that need healing. Write them down and take those things to God in prayer.

Say this Prayer

God, lead me on the road of healing.

Amen

Grace

Reflection

_____

_____

_____

_____

_____

_____

_____

_____

_____

_____

_____

_____

_____

_____

_____

_____

_____

_____

GRACE

Pray for your closet friend. Speak life into their dreams and aspirations.

Say this Prayer

God, may my prayers be a fountain of life for someone else.

Amen